THE YOGI POEMS
and other celebrations
of local baseball

THE YOGI POEMS
and other celebrations of local baseball

Raphael Badagliacca

iUniverse, Inc.
New York   Bloomington

The Yogi Poems and other Celebrations of Local Baseball

iUniverse books may be ordered through booksellers or by contacting:

iUniverse
1663 Liberty Drive
Bloomington, IN 47403
www.iuniverse.com
1-800-Authors (1-800-288-4677)

Because of the dynamic nature of the Internet, any Web addresses or links contained in this book may have changed since publication and may no longer be valid. The views expressed in this work are solely those of the author and do not necessarily reflect the views of the publisher, and the publisher hereby disclaims any responsibility for them.

ISBN: 978-1-4401-2033-6 (pbk)
ISBN: 978-1-4401-2034-3 (ebk)

Printed in the United States of America

iUniverse rev. date: 3/2/2009

for the man in the back of the room

THE YOGI POEMS
and other celebrations
of local baseball

GAME ONE

The Lineup

1 Yogi: Bartlett's Only MVP 1
2 Rivalry 3
3 Yogi: Perfect. 7
4 Saint Yogi 9
5 Most Valuable Player 11
6 Yogi: Words 15
7 Syzygy. 17
8 The Alumni Game 21
9 Playoff 23

GAME TWO

The Lineup

1 Yogi 27
2 Aunt Jean 29
3 Soap Opera 31
4 There is a Season 33
5 Tiger Stadium 39
6 Holy Orders 43
7 Heartland 49
8 Tickets 51
9 Bat and Ball 53

EXTRA INNINGS

1 Yogi: Swing Music 55
2 Alexander the Great 57
3 Winter Ball 59
4 Reunion 65
5 10 o'clock 69
6 Mr. November 71
7 ∞ 75

Bartlett's Only MVP

Shakespeare shaped the language.
Some say he invented it.
Wilde and Shaw spun expressions of unrelenting wit.
Whitman taught the mother tongue
How to sing for us;
Yeats scaled the beauty of her lonely peaks.
Joyce uncovered something new,
And so did Eliot.

But unlike Yogi, none of them could hit.

Rivalry

I was astonished to learn that the 2008 baseball season would mark the thirtieth anniversary of Bucky Dent's famous home-run. On the day of that event, I had just completed a nine-month assignment to write a dictionary for IBM. I had just spent the last night in my rented upstate house. I had just sold my car because I knew I would no longer need it back in my true home, New York City. I stopped for a moment in a local bar in Woodstock to check out the score of the game. I ended up staying for all nine innings.

A small, black and white television hung above the bar. The place was filled with the usual Woodstock populace, mostly long-haired, bearded men. I had lived among them for nearly a year, slipping away to my 9-5 corporate job. I was surprised to discover the baseball fans. As the game progressed, single emotions would ripple down the bar – groans or cheers – until the crescendo moment when everyone broke ranks, backs were slapped, and I believed I saw a few tears. I left that bar with the feeling that anything was possible, that you could make up a 14-game deficit, that a small man could accomplish a big thing. Bus ticket in hand, I crossed the street.

There were two women seated in front of me on the bus. The little boy with them stood in the aisle. He had a baseball glove on his hand, and he was wearing a Boston Red Sox hat that looked just a little too large for his head. He had freckles. I guessed he was about eight years old.

I could only see the backs of the women's heads. The woman on my left hand, nearer the aisle, had brown curly hair with a kerchief on top. The woman on the window side of the seat also had brown hair, but it was totally straight, and redder than the other woman's hair.

The woman with the curly hair did most of the talking. She bobbed her head when she spoke, so that it almost seemed as if the thoughts were springing from the coiled launching pads of so many curls.

The other woman was younger. She looked to be in her late twenties or early thirties. The boy belonged to her.

"So you've never been to the city," the talkative woman said. "It's a great place," she promptly announced, "but you've got to keep your wits about you."

The younger head nodded.

The bus was moving through the greenery of upstate New York, on its way to the humming steadiness of the thruway, where only an occasional rock formation would break the visual monotony.

"You'll be arriving in the Port Authority," said the bobbing head. "Not a pretty place."

"We're only making a connection there," the young woman said.

"Oh," said the curly head. "So you're not really going to the city?"

"No," said the younger woman, but she didn't reveal her final destination.

"That's much worse."

"Why?"

"Because you'll be in that godforsaken Port Authority for who knows how long while you wait for your next bus…"

The boy was in his own world. He was rocking back and forth on the balls of his feet and humming to himself. He seemed to have made a game out of exaggerating the movements of the bus, as if they occasionally threatened to throw him to the floor. He would swing around and right himself, conquering every imaginary curve.

"Yes, it's a crazy place the Big Apple. No telling who's walking around, especially when it gets dark."

The younger woman nodded, but didn't say anything.

There was a long silence, in which I thought the older woman might have fallen asleep. We were making very good time. Traffic was surprisingly light. Soon the skyline came into sight. Soon the buildings burst into existence all around us.

The curly head shook itself and the familiar voice repeated its cautions all over again, more vehemently the deeper we made our way into the heart of the city.

"Now, remember," she said "you have to be careful. You don't know who you're dealing with. It's New York. You have to be very careful."

"Yeah," the boy with the Red Sox hat said in a surprisingly loud voice. "All those Yankee fans!"

Perfect

There is nothing as perfect as nothing.

Not since the Babylonian invented it,
had nine instances of zero
been put to better use.

According to all accounts,
it was a perfect day for baseball.

The Don of all the universe let go the spinning sphere
and for all eternity, Yogi caught it clear.

When the ball bounced off of Carey
into McDougald's hands
no one in the crowded stands
could grasp the meaning of that play.

But in the fifth, when Mantle made
a running catch that saved the day
sixty-four thousand five hundred nineteen
suddenly became aware of nothing.

Nothing brought them to their feet.
Nothing made them gasp.
Nothing made them bite their lips.
Nothing kept them on the edges of their seats.

As they tracked the movements of the ball,
They dreamt a single dream of nothing at all.

And this dream transformed them into witnesses.

When the final pitch was thrown
down through the years,

ending two careers
umpire and batter
would never see another,

a monumental silence fell,
as before an awesome work of nature.

Then Yogi broke the spell.

Timeless are the moments when
Perfection is achieved by imperfect men.

Saint Yogi

There were five Roman Catholic churches within a mile of our "new" house in the suburbs, but we didn't know this in the first week of our arrival, only days before Christmas. I put *new* in quotation marks because the house was built in 1908. None of these five churches, by the way, is in our town.

Snow was predicted upon our arrival. I moved the car to the end of the driveway. I didn't know if I would find a snow shovel in the garage, and by the time the weather bulletin appeared on television, it was already dark. We came from the city and owned nothing as useful as a flashlight, so even if I wanted to search the garage for a shovel, I wouldn't be able to see anything.

It did snow the next morning, and it continued to snow for a few days, but lightly, just enough to reinforce the Christmas feeling.

On Christmas morning, we entered the first church we found. During the mass, when the priest exhorts the members of the congregation to give each other the sign of peace, I turned around to see our four-year old son shaking the hand of Yogi Berra, hall of fame catcher, local hero, and source of endless good sense.

That's how we came to choose our parish.

Most Valuable Player

My son asked me if it was possible to pray for something not to happen.

He was a seven-year old boy kneeling at the foot of his bed just learning how to say his prayers.

"Sure," I said. And then he prayed to God in his infinite mercy to prevent the 1994 major league baseball strike from continuing into the 1995 season. Then he turned to me and asked if I would coach his baseball team this year.

My team had boys and girls on it. This would be the first year they would face pitched balls, instead of hitting off the tee. Coaches pitched to their own teams. There was a guideline that if a child did not hit the ball in a certain number of pitches the tee should be brought out, but I paid no attention to it. As the pitcher-coach, I considered it my job to study each errant swing and aim the ball at the bat. We didn't use the tee once.

Before the first practice, I sat everyone down on the grass. From how they were holding their gloves, I saw that we would have to begin with basics, like the difference between right-handed and left-handed.

"How do we know which hand to put our gloves on?" I said.

"I know," one boy said, matter-of-factly. "It's the hand you don't color with."

There was a rule that you had to change everyone's position each inning, so that no player spent too much time in the outfield. This meant that the whole team would gather around me whenever we were about to take the field, each one begging for an infield position. It got so that I made one of my own rules – you could end up playing any position except the one you requested. It didn't take long for everyone to start asking to play the outfield.

I relented once. One of the boys jumped up and down, shouting, "I want to play shortstop! I want to play shortstop! Let me be shortstop!"

"Alright," I said. "Play shortstop."

"Where *is* that?" he asked.

Baseball at this level is a different game. An out is the rarest of things. There were two ways to retire the side – the traditional three outs, which almost never happened, and a complete run-through of the batting order. Runs were plentiful. So were overthrows, and misplays of every kind. It would have been more accurate to change the way scoring is kept by crediting a team with the number of outs it got in the field instead of the number of runs it scored. We didn't keep score, but so many runners crossed the plate that the members of both teams left each game convinced they had won.

We had other peculiarities. From time to time, I would find one of my players crying: standing in the outfield; in the on-deck circle with a batting helmet firmly in place; alone on the bench, curiously separate from the rest of the players. I always asked what might be wrong in an understanding tone. If the reason was something physical and minor, this was always a relief. But usually the source remained mysterious, even to the player, it seemed.

One boy threw his glove on top of the backstop once every game, while two others, full of energy, scrambled up the chain links in a race to retrieve it. These were sub-dramas, like the events happening in the corner of a painting by Breughel.

One player emerged.

If it's possible for a seven-year old to possess management skills, she did. First, she knew the game. She knew what a force play was, and not to leave the base when an infielder might catch a line drive or a pop-up. These were major achievements.

On this small playing field, she had mastered the fundamentals – she could hit, hit with power, run, throw and field – but her talents did not have so much to do with physical size or experience as they did with intense focus. In a game where no score was kept she became upset with herself and others whenever a performance could have been better. She would come to me with suggestions about re-positioning the players in the field. She willed perfection.

The crowning moment came in the last game. With runners on first and second, a ground ball was hit to shortstop. She fielded it cleanly, tagged the runner on second as he ran by, stepped on second base to force the runner on first, and then threw the ball to our shaky first baseman who caught it this time to complete the triple play – a remarkable outcome even at the major league level.

After the game, I carried the equipment to the car for the last time. I threw away the carton that held the new baseballs now that none were left. The kids were passing with their parents. They waved good-bye and I waved back. Some of them came forward to thank me, and I thanked them for a great season.

When she arrived, I told her and her father what a great player she was and what a great future she had. What I was really thinking was not the kind of thing I would say because it sounded too corny, too much like a self-help aphorism. Even mentioning the future seemed out of place.

Yet I wanted a seven-year old girl to know that the independence and the confidence she exuded was a precious gift that needed nurturing.

The season that had begun for me with a prayer was ending with a mantra, even if I could not say it out loud: *Be your own MVP.*

Words

You were right, Number 8.
It gets late early out here.
No matter how long the days may seem
The years accelerate
And some time in the afternoon
The shadow falls.

If the world were perfect, it wouldn't be.
So use the hours that you have
To live here and now,
Not in some dream of perfection
A bigger house, a more attractive mate.
Take the pitch that's thrown to you
Even if it's off the plate
And drive it for a double.

It's deja-vu all over again
That feeling that you've been here before
Feeling this exact feeling
That you're not getting anywhere.
Where is there to get
Except to a place within yourself
Go back to fundamentals
Throw the ball to the right base.

It ain't over till it's over
So don't give up before the contest ends
But don't slack off, either
Once it's done, it's done
All talk of might have beens
Will not undo the winning run.

If wisdom were to wrap itself in words,
What better words than these.

Syzygy

Night in the town where we live is especially dark. This is because the streets are not electrified. Instead, we have gas lamps.

The gas lamps give the town a feeling of elegance, but they don't give much light. The combination of low light and uneven sidewalks has sent more than one new resident sprawling. The standing joke is that you need a miner's hat with a beacon to keep from falling. Many a pizza delivery boy has spent precious minutes hopelessly searching for the right house while the pie cooled off.

For a few hours on one evening, a celestial event changed all of this.

In our house, we had just moved into a new phase called adolescence. In this phase, the predictable becomes unpredictable. Speech is replaced by awkward silences. Gestures of affection, especially in public, are suddenly off limits. The worst thing a parent can do is attempt to say something funny in a car full of teenage friends. It will soon be made clear that as driver your job is to drive to the destination without saying a single word, like the man with the top hat in a hansom cab.

Parents experiencing adolescence undergo physical changes. They begin to feel old, so old that they can't remember their own adolescences. They're prone to exaggeration and wild mood swings. They begin to doubt themselves and ask if they are the only ones feeling these massive changes.

For me, one change symbolized everything – my son was ambivalent about having a catch. How many times had we taken out the ball and two gloves in his short life – two hundred, five hundred, a thousand?

I remember a variation where we tossed an orange in the kitchen, stealthily, underhandedly, because his mother had announced – no ball playing in the house!

How many times had he come to me with the question: "Wanna have a catch?" I always wanted to have a catch. Throwing a baseball was for me one of the most life-affirming acts on the globe. Each throw recognized our separateness, each catch confirmed our connection.

We threw softballs, hardballs, tennis balls, a cloth ball we called the crooked ball, even a frisbee on occasion. We kept track of our streaks – how many throws we could make without dropping the ball. He asked me to throw him hard grounders, and he responded with spectacular leaping throws to my first baseman's stance. He asked me to throw him high pop-ups, which I did the way my cousin had shown me many years ago, looking up and throwing overhand.

There may have been one or two or a dozen times in his life when I was too preoccupied to say, "Yes, I'll have a catch with you," and now I regret every one of them, but not as much as I regret the day I came to him and said, "Wanna have a catch?" and he answered me with: "That's alright," which in his new, relaxed lingo meant simply "No." I was devastated.

The dictionary defines *syzygy* as an event in which three or more celestial bodies are in perfect alignment. On one night in the recent past, the northeastern United States experienced a syzygy and our town, one of the darkest places in the universe, was flooded with light at 9:30PM.

Earlier in the evening, I had persuaded my son to come out at the appointed time to see something he might never see again. Once out, we did something it seemed as if we had not done since the mornings in New York City when I would bring him to pre-school. We went for a walk.

It only lasted five minutes, but it was full of a sense of discovery under that impossible light, just as it had been back then, when we ran from the two-headed monster drainpipes, avoided the cracks in the sidewalk, and jumped up from the street over each curb with both feet together.

We found ourselves back in front of the house. The same thought rushed to our lips: "Wanna have a catch?"

And so we did, adding a fourth celestial body to the perfect alignment of this evening – the orb traveling between us.

The Alumni Game

This will be a bittersweet year for the high school baseball team. The team is full of promise. Six of the starting varsity players are seniors who have been playing at this level since their sophomore year. There is more and better pitching this year than in any we can remember. This year everything points to a winning season.

Most of the seniors also played football. That this was their last football season seemed to take them unaware until the final few games, but that experience has informed this one, and they go into this baseball season not only knowing, but also feeling from the start that this will be the last time they play together.

The feeling extends beyond the field into the stands. The six seniors are the only boys in their families. Six fathers, passionate and well meaning fans, also go into their final season.

It was with these thoughts in mind that I arrived early for the annual alumni game, which opens the season. In this game, alumni, recent and not so recent, play the current high school squad. Usually, the alumni play their hearts out. For the high school team, this game is their first chance to air out their arms and practice their strokes in preparation for the coming season; for the alumni, this game is their season.

I am not an alumnus of our town's high school, so I could hardly expect to play, but I just happened to have my glove and my spikes in the car. So when it seemed as if the alumni team might not have enough players, I just happened to be standing there. After happily agreeing to fill in, I walked slowly to the car but my heart was leaping at the prospect of stepping onto the field again.

I played third base. You might consider the hot corner, where a line drive can be on you in an instant, a dangerous choice for someone "slightly" out of practice. I think of third base as pure instinct. And instincts stay with you, no matter what.

I played through my youth as a shortstop, where instinct is also important, of course, but range is really the thing. Over the shoulder catches in the outfield, hard ground balls hit deep into the hole, longer throws, stolen bases, pivots and double plays – by contrast, third base is a quiet place, an alligator dozing in the heat, ready to snap without notice.

My only concern was the bunt. But when I looked at the kids, swinging the bat for the first time after the long winter, I felt sure that no one had bunting in mind.

I took my position and with it came some razzing from the fans, my friends. "What are you going to do," the third-base coach said, "if he hits it your way?" He was referring to my son, who had just stepped into the batter's box.

"Throw him out," I said. "Just like anyone else."

He took the first pitch for a strike. He took the next two for balls. Each time I touched the ground with my glove – easier to come up than go down – ready for a line drive or a bouncing ball that might come my way, no matter how hard.

Instead, he stroked the next pitch deep into right center field, an ever-increasing arc, high over the heads of the scrambling outfielders, much farther than I could have ever hit a ball. As he rounded the bases, I found myself clapping, drawing the attention of my teammates. He passed me in a hurry, touching all four bases well ahead of the throw.

Suddenly, I understood. We were playing the alumni game. As parents, we played it every day. With every pitch we hoped they would hit the ball farther than we ever could. And if we could be there to see it happen, the reward would be even greater.

Playoff

Someone had scratched out part of the letter "N" in the word "NO" on the sign at the entrance to the park; instead of "No Dogs Allowed," it read "10 Dogs Allowed."

Maybe that explained why there were two dogs nosing around behind the backstop. A silver cat watched them from her regal perch atop the stone wall.

It was the beginning of the end of the summer. The traveling baseball teams that had played well enough were still in the game. On this particular night two of those teams would meet each other in a playoff, and the winners' summer would continue just a little bit longer than the losers'.

The players' mothers and siblings took their seats in the metallic stands. The fathers would trickle in as the evening proceeded, in shirt sleeves or suit coats, some carrying briefcases. The younger brothers and sisters of the players clearly did not grasp the importance of the moment. The older sisters found their friends, and from the rhythm of their speech, you could tell that they were happy to be here, but you also got the feeling that their noisy exuberance might have nothing to do with the game about to be played.

The home team was just finishing its warm-ups. The umpire whisked off the plate and rose to his full height, looking through the backstop at the seated fans. He had the physique of a player himself. He turned around, shouted "Play ball!" and put on his mask, getting down to business.

The first batter drove the second pitch of the game deep into center field where the outfielder planted himself under it and made the catch. With only two pitches thrown, the tempo had been set, and every spectator who had endured the season could see why these two teams of thirteen year olds had made it this far. Their play was several cuts above that of their contemporaries.

Every parent hung on every pitch, except for one woman. She was deeply absorbed in reading a book.

She had long, blond hair that hid her face from a side view. She was slim, had a summer tan, and wore a yellow, sleeveless top and blue jean shorts. I had never seen her before.

I ran through the list of players to try to determine whose mother she could possibly be. It made sense that someone too busy to attend any of the season's games might show up now that the team was fighting for a championship. But it didn't make sense that she would display such disinterest. I imagined her son begging her to come, and she complying technically, without ever looking up from her book.

It was a hard cover book that looked to be well over 500 pages long. She had read a little more than half of it. She seemed totally absorbed in every sentence. She had it open on one knee, the other leg sometimes dangling down to the next row, sometimes pairing itself up so her two knees touched.

I decided that I had to do two things: see her face and find out what book she was reading.

I leaned as far as I dared from my seat two rows up from hers. The title was repeated at the top of every right-hand page. From where I sat I could see the word "After..." but no more.

By now two innings had ended and the game was scoreless. Both pitchers were right on the money, and the play behind them had been sparkling.

I thought I saw the word "the" after "After." "After the..."

The ping of the bat and the sudden bursts of cheers from everyone sitting all around her did not make her raise her head. Neither did the barking and snarling of the two dogs who had somehow managed to cross each other after an hour of harmony. They were only ten feet from her and yet she still did not look up from her book.

I made my way down the stands and walked over to the water fountain, so that I could come back and glance at her face. The home team scored on a triple followed by a sacrifice fly. This brought the hometown crowd to its feet twice, with high-fives and backslapping, except for her. She remained seated and turned the next page.

She was a good-looking woman, with regular features and a fresh complexion. Maybe she was an aunt visiting for the day. Or maybe a baby-sitter for one of the younger siblings. No, a baby-sitter would have looked up at least once or twice to make sure that her charge was still in the park. How could anyone be so neutral?

Why would anyone so uninvolved in the game choose to sit here to read her book? There were so many more attractive benches throughout the town in less noisy, more secluded spots. There were the benches around the pond where the only sound was the occasional quack from a duck. Why not sit there? I began to feel sorry for the player she had come to see, whoever that was.

After seven innings the score was tied at 2. The game went into extra innings. Pending darkness arrived to influence the outcome. In the bottom of the second extra inning, the home team rallied, putting together three straight singles and winning the game on a dramatic play at the plate which sent dirt flying in all directions. The umpire gestured and loudly pronounced the runner safe. The winning team ran on the field to embrace the batter and congratulate themselves. The fans cheered and clapped. Only the woman reading the book didn't look up.

We all went off to our cars, some with light steps and smiling faces, and others looking dejected and dragging their feet. I drove down the narrow road past the umpire who had his trunk wide open. He had just removed his chest protector when she came up, threw her arms around him, and they kissed warmly. He was still holding the mask, but she had dropped her book so that it fell into the street with the pages open.

Yogi

Now that we've grown up
You are the one we want to be
Always steady under pressure
Famous for coming through
Quoted by senators and presidents
Comfortable in your celebrity,
Wearing it like an old shoe.

Aunt Jean

Aunt Jean is my godmother. She reminds me of this every time I see her. In vivid detail, she recounts how she and my godfather, Uncle Angelo, carried me through the streets of Brooklyn on the day of my christening. "We had no cars then," she always says, and I look down and see the cobblestones as if they are there right now, beneath my feet.

Aunt Jean is a character. She makes friends easily. Strangers warm up to her. She can be loud and uninhibited in the most positive ways. She loosens up the crowd. Everyone loves her.

Uncle Angelo was quieter. He loved sports and gambling for small stakes. He excelled at games of skill, like pool and bocce. He loved anything that involved a ball or a horse. He was a fan of the races.

He also loved the Yankees. He knew about every player going seven decades back. He spoke often about DiMaggio and Mantle and Maris, about Reggie and his favorite pitcher, Guidry, which he pronounced, "Jid-dree," softening the sound of the G.

He expressed the intense desire to meet, just once, Yogi and Rizzuto. Both men lived only towns away from me, and I had met them separately at different times in public forums. It is one of my great regrets that I never devised a way to make this meeting happen for my uncle.

He was a fan with longevity. The players of each period were alive in his mind, each in their prime, getting the game-winning hit, making the impossible catch, striking out the side.

In what would turn out to be the last week of his life, before a scheduled operation, I see him gallantly showing my aunt some of the things she might need to know, like how to pump gas at the self-service station, something she has never done before. It is the ultimate act of chivalry. At age 84, he patiently stands there, full head of white hair, as she completes the task under his supervision.

Aunt Jean has always been an early riser. For years, she has called us every Saturday morning. Her call announces the day. If I pick up, she talks briefly with me. She expresses concern about my work, and then moves to my wife for the week's conversation.

Aunt Jean has never been a sports fan. Her only sport was shopping, bargain hunting to be more exact. It was rumored that she bought and stocked items in multiples and kept them for years. People said her basement resembled a warehouse. At one of the department stores where she worked, the manager would ask her for certain items from her inventory to fill the shelves on thin days.

I wish I could do more for my godmother. I know she's lonely. But she's also fiercely independent. I've invited her to come and stay with us. I've offered to drive out to pick her up, to take her anywhere she might want to go.

Here's how she changes the subject: "What do you think of the Yanks' chances this year? Is it going to happen?"

or "Will they ever give Jeter the MVP? At least Phil's in the Hall of Fame."

I think it's her way of letting me know that she's not really so alone.

Any day now, I expect her to tell me about the most accomplished single season in pitching history: "25 wins, only 3 losses. 19 strikeouts in one game. Jid-dree! Louisiana Lightning!"

Soap Opera

One day, when he was about two years old, my son and I crossed the street together just outside our city apartment and entered Riverside Park.

There were two paths you could take – one led downwards under the shade of elegant trees. Impressive rocks gathered in a cluster since a time before there were any buildings across the street or anywhere.

The upward path took you to a small field of grass and stone benches. Sunlight was everywhere. Beyond the wall, you could see the river and the buildings on the opposite shore.

I handed my son a yellow whiffle bat, and set him up on the edge of the field in the batter's position, with his back to the river. From a distance of five or six large steps away, I pitched a plastic ball underhand. He swung and missed. He was a little boy with a dark, incredibly curly head.

"Are you ready?" I said, and pitched the second ball. He swung and missed.

I walked over to him and gently took the bat from his hands.

"This way," I said, smoothly swinging the bat in one even motion. I handed the bat back to him.

I went back to my pitcher's position. I pitched the ball. He swung and missed. I pitched again. He swung and missed. Before each new pitch, I paused, and said: "Are you ready?"

After the twentieth pitch, he had still not made contact with the ball.

"Are you ready?" I said, and pitched again. This time he swung and the ball came rapidly back at me – a line drive that hit me in the upper chest and bounced away. I heard clapping and cheering.

I turned around to see five members of the cast of the soap opera *All My Children*, who had been watching us from the path. A white-haired actor stood in front of the group, leading the cheer.

Whenever I'm switching channels and see his face fill the screen, I stop long enough to find out how his character is being tested at that moment, and think back to this day.

There is a Season

From the trunk of the car I took the usual items and one more: glove, bat, new ball still in the box, scorebook, and this time, the digital camera. This was our first playoff game and possibly our last game of the season, and I wanted a picture of the team that almost wasn't.

The team had been in existence for 20 years. I had played ever since we moved to the town, thirteen years ago. Never once in all that time had we come close to forfeiting a game, but this year, at the outset, it just did not seem like we had enough to field a team. Injured knees and family obligations had depleted our numbers. This was the over-thirty league, and most of us were in our forties.

At the last minute, we appealed to the town police. Four officers wanted to play. They explained that they alternated shifts on Sundays and that we could expect to see two of them each week. On the day of the first game, two passersby in the park expressed interest in playing. One was an urban type, wearing dark glasses with his ear almost always glued to a cell phone. The other looked bookish; even though he stood there in sweats and a baseball hat, you imagined him wearing a suit and a striped tie. He explained to us how much he liked the sport, that he had talented voice, that he sometimes sang the star spangled banner for the local minor league team. It was an uneven collection of players that grew into a team and finished the regular season with a respectable record. After all here we were, about to enter the playoffs.

During batting practice I went to third base where I knew I would play this game. On a sleepy Sunday morning, third base in slow-pitch softball is an efficient place to rapidly wake up. It was more like tennis than baseball. I'm proud to say that nothing got by me, in the practice or the game.

Coming off the field, I quickly decided that trying to take the picture before the game would be a mistake. We needed every ounce of concentration we could summon for the contest; besides, the act of taking the photo would seem to imply that I felt that we would not survive the single elimination to take the photo next week. I'd wait until the end of the game.

We went down in order in the top of the first inning. They scored twice in the bottom of the inning. In the top of the second, our fifth batter doubled. I was batting sixth. Years ago, I had learned how to hit the ball to any field; it was the defensive strategy of a spray hitter without much power. I surveyed the field from my position in the batter's box and decided that right-center field would give me the best opportunity to drop in a single and score the runner. I hit the ball exactly where I wanted it to go, but instead of falling in front of the outfielder, it took off and soared over his head. As I rounded first base, I saw his back as he ran after the ball. As I approached the third base coach, he was actually waving me home. No one in the entire park was more astonished than me. I crossed the plate with the first home run of my career and the score was tied.

Hitting a homerun is different. No matter how much you may think or say a hit is a hit and getting on base is all that matters, a homerun feels different. It is the perfect harmony of bat, ball and swing; it feels entirely smooth and connected, like something that was meant to be, maybe like all things that are meant to be.

The game see sawed. They went ahead 4-2. We went ahead 6-4. I got a second hit, a single this time. They tied it at 6. Then, in what would become their last at-bat, they shot ahead with 8 runs. It was nobody's fault; it was just how softball scoring went. After trying to eke out a walk, I made the first out of our last inning with a fly ball to center field.

I asked the captain of the other team to take our picture. Everyone lined up. He pointed and clicked, but nothing happened. He tried again. "Is the battery dead?" he asked. Regardless, I knew the moment had passed; I couldn't get them to pose again; a loss made everyone want to leave the field in a hurry.

We all shook hands and congratulated each other on a great season. I gathered up the same items I had carried from the car before the game, except for the ball, and walked back to the parking lot. There I saw two of our players talking to an elderly man. As I approached, they addressed me.

"He's looking for a field," one of the guys said, "where his grandson played last week. He thought it was here, but it isn't. He says there were several fields together."

"A lot of fields," the old man said.

"Brookdale," I suggested.

"Yeah, Brookdale," they agreed. It was somewhat out of the way – the largest park in the area, with a track, soccer fields, at least five softball fields, even a dog run."

"How do I get there?" the old man asked.

They both began to give him directions, and I saw a bewildered look come over his face.

"I can take you there," I said.

"Okay," he answered. "I'll follow you."

We had about three miles to cover. I took him through many streets, checking every so often to make sure I hadn't lost him. I stopped at every yellow light. When we finally entered the secluded expanse of the park with its tremendous trees and colorful bicyclists, I pulled over and he dutifully came to a stop behind me. Even before he lowered the window, I could see him shaking his head no.

"This is not it," he said.

"Are you sure?" I asked. "There are several fields just around the bend."

"No," he nodded. "I don't recognize anything."

"Then where could it possibly be," I wondered, aloud, and then I asked, "How old is your grandson?"

I thought the image of 12 or 15-year olds might make the connection for me.

"It's my son I've come to see," he corrected me. "He has a make-up double-header because the field was too wet to play last week. I can't believe how late I am."

"How old is your son?" I asked.

"My son is sixty-six years old."

He must be in his late eighties, I thought. Maybe he's ninety. It moved me that he had driven out to see his sixty-six year old boy's double-header, and how anxious he was about missing the beginning.

"It starts at 10 o'clock," he said.

"Does your son have a cell phone?" I asked. "I could call him."

He nodded no.

"What about calling his house? Maybe his wife has the schedule."

"I can't remember the number," he said. "I can't remember anything," he said, in a regretful voice.

"Are you sure it was this week?" I asked. "It didn't rain last week. It rained the week before. The field was wet when we played two weeks ago. Are you sure the double-header is this week?"

"I'm sure," he said, and then, "I don't want to take up any more of your day. You've got things to do."

"It's okay," I said.   If we found the game, I was now considering watching an inning or two. Maybe it was an over-sixty league.

He mentioned a certain road and asked me to take him back there. From there, he would drive to his son's house and ask his daughter-in-law if she knew where the games were being played. "Although I doubt it," he added.

I walked back to the car and led him through the streets in the direction he wanted to go.   After a mile or two, I pulled over again with the thought of asking him one or two more questions, but he assumed I had arrived at my destination and waved to me as he drove by.

"Good luck," I said as he slowly moved out of sight, but in a voice that only I could hear, and suddenly it struck me that I did not have a father anymore.

Inexplicably, the lens of the digital camera zoomed out. So it does work, I thought. Next year, I'll check the battery.

Tiger Stadium

After I got over the fact that neither of the local teams would make an appearance in the 2006 World Series, I began to root for the Tigers. I did this out of nostalgia for the year 1983, the year before the magical 35-5 start when Detroit went all the way to defeat the Padres and become world champions. In 1983, the team came in second place.

That year, I worked at a large NYC advertising agency with a Detroit office. I did all of the background work and wrote the copy for a major scientific campaign on the basic research conducted by one of the nation's major automobile manufacturers. I was expected to make a trip to the labs located in a Detroit suburb to interview the scientists once a month, and to produce three-page ads from those interviews that ran in some of the world's most scientific journals.

The scientists were much like artists, except that their canvases were sometimes as small as the orbit of an electron, sometimes as big as the sky. Their areas of exploration were only tangentially related to automobiles. I wrote about the world's strongest magnet for its tiny mass. I wrote about the inevitable invisible cracks that develop in the strongest steel over time. I wrote about the behavior of gases in the air; a reader wrote back to ask on which side of the highway he should build his church to best avoid pollution. I wrote about an innovative, rapid way to solve non-linear polynomial equations; thousands of letters came in asking for the original paper with the magical formula; a coal company told us they could use the method to locate minors trapped underground.

In the spring, pitchers and catchers reported to camp, and everything was right with the world again. On one of my visits to Detroit I learned that the automobile company had been forced to lay off thousands of workers, and that they were reluctant to sit in their usual box at Tiger Stadium. This season's tickets had been given to our agency.

You cannot get closer to the field in any major league park than you could in old Tiger Stadium. Sometimes, the batter on deck got in the way.

The first few games I felt sorry for the batters. After all of my years of playing and watching baseball I never imagined how fast a fast ball could be or how much a curve ball could possibly curve.

A few line drives through the box adjusted my attitude. I was amazed by the ferocity with which some balls flew off the bat, and surprised that more pitchers and third basemen did not leave the field on stretchers. I began to think of a hit as a sure thing from the moment it left the bat, except for those rare instances when a fielder happened to be standing in the way.

I kept score at the games. Anyone who can decipher the hieroglyphic symbols of the scoring system can recreate all of the action that took place in any game regardless of how many years have passed. It gave me an unequalled feeling of calm and control to keep score. I would happily do it for five or so games in a row, and then it would make me just as happy to take a break and not do it for the next game.

While I was sitting at my desk in New York, the head of the laboratories would sometimes call me to go over the research projects I had reviewed, and ask for my recommendations. The ideal topic had to be ground-breaking and significant, but not so proprietary that announcing it to the world in this way would be premature.

He would ask me when I would be visiting next. I would always say that I had to consult my schedule, which was my Detroit Tigers schedule. I brought it down from the bulletin board and tracing the dates with my finger I always agreed to a series of days that would give me the maximum number of games.

One morning, the head of our Detroit office called and asked me to pay a visit on a certain day. An important client would be coming in from out of town, and he wanted me to meet him. I had never had a request like this before.

When I arrived, two of our account executives met me at the airport. This had never happened before.

As we drove from the airport to the office, they explained that the visiting client was a big baseball fan. They had invited him to the game that night and they wanted me to be there, too.

"And make sure you keep score," one of them said.

We arrived at the tail end of batting practice. The client knew his baseball. He complimented the two account executives on the excellence of the seats.

When the Tigers took the field, he said to me, "That's why this team is going to win games – strength up the middle." He pointed to Parrish setting up behind the plate and Trammel and Whitaker standing near second base. Jack Morris was on the mound.

The account executives were very solicitous towards their charge. If he cheered, they cheered. If he made a remark of any kind, they both nodded their heads.

At one point in the early innings, the client suddenly stood up. The two account executives looked at each other and stood up as well.

The client began to shout excitedly and motion with his hand. "Look! A bat! A bat!"

From the look on their faces, it occurred to the account executives in a flash that the client had lost his mind. We were, after all, at a baseball game. But this look was quickly replaced by one of confusion as they tried to reconcile their feelings with their mission, which was above all to be agreeable.

"A bat! A bat!" the client repeated loudly.

To our surprise, a furry creature flew in a graceful arc above our heads and disappeared into the darkness of the night.

Holy Orders

There is a time near the end of the summer when the heat rises to embrace his cool morning mistress before setting out to do the day's scorching work. The result is near perfection in the air.

It was one of those Sunday mornings. I was standing on the driveway, taking in the air like nectar, looking at my watch, holding my spiked shoes, my glove, and my workbook for lectors. It was ten minutes to nine.

Some time ago, one of the nuns at the church had approached and asked if I would serve as a Eucharistic minister. Twelve years of catholic school in another era, much closer in sentiment to the Middle Ages, had left its impression. I could not imagine myself handling the host, let alone dispensing it to parishioners.

I declined by saying, "I'd rather do the reading."

"It's not reading," she said. "It's proclaiming the word."

That's how I became a lector, with the responsibility once a month to proclaim the word at nine o'clock mass.

The Liturgical Calendar is an ancient thing. It begins with anticipation and ends with celebration and then begins all over again. The softball schedule is more linear. It starts with a feeling of renewal for sure, it pounds through the dead heat of the summer, and it ends in a round of single loss elimination playoffs.

As each summer approaches, I match the two schedules and go about exchanging assignments with the other lectors to avoid the weeks when we have a nine o'clock game.

This was not one of those weeks. This week the game would begin at 10:30. It was do-or-die playoff time.

I put the spikes and glove in the back seat of the car, on top of my team shirt and sweatpants, and drove to the church.

The words themselves never posed a problem for me. They always told a story and telling a story came naturally. I had a little trouble at first with the footwork, when to come up the front side of the altar to the podium, when to go around the back, when to bow, when to exit down the aisle. That first performance I was uncertain whether to bow before placing the heavy book on the altar, so I half-bowed and glided away in the same motion.

"Good with the Word," the nun had said to me afterwards, "but what was that little curtsy in front of the altar?"

I parked the car just in time. Once inside the church, I picked up the book in its gold colored metal casing, and joined the procession down to the altar.

The first reading happens fairly soon. This was a Sunday in what the calendar called Ordinary Time. I read from the book of Proverbs:

"Wisdom has built her house,
    she has set up her seven columns,
  she has dressed her meat, mixed her wine,
    yes, she has spread her table…
'Let whoever is simple turn in here';
    to the one who lacks understanding, she says,
'Come eat of my food,
    and drink of the wine I have mixed…'

When I finished the reading I took a seat behind the podium, and watched the cantor walk over from the organ. She stood in the spot I had just occupied, with her back to me. Her hair was exceedingly black falling down from her shoulders. As the music rose, the beauty of her voice transported me to a different time and place, to a French cathedral, to a story I found myself constructing out of bits and pieces

Victor Hugo must have discarded, involving love and intrigue. It abruptly ended when the music stopped.

I stood for the second reading, a letter from St. Paul:

"Brothers and sisters:
  When that which is mortal clothes itself with immortality,
    then the word that was written shall come about:
    Death is swallowed up in victory.
    Where, O death is your victory?
    Where, O death is your sting?..."

At communion time, I left my lector's seat to take the host from my friend Dan, our team shortstop, who, braver than me, had accepted the Eucharistic assignment. I said my "Amen," giving the slightest nod of recognition. In a short while we would be on the field together.

The Mass went on longer than expected. There were special announcements at the end. I fought the impulse to look at my watch.

The announcements came to an end. The three altar girls crossed the floor to get the two large candles and the cross. I joined them between the rows of pews, facing the altar. The priest kissed the altar, our cue to turn and begin the measured procession towards the back of the church, while the organ music rose.

Once outside the church, I walked quickly towards the parking lot. I saw Dan ahead of me, in another quadrant, crossing the street hurriedly. By the time I reached the lot, he was standing against his car, peeling off his clothes to the astonishment of passersby. Somehow, he'd managed to fit his team shirt and more underneath his suit.

He drove off before I even reached my car. I had about seven minutes to reach the field. I kicked off my shoes while I drove, shedding articles of clothing without slowing down and shoving them across to the floor on the passenger side.

As I pulled into the parking lot beyond right field, I saw the last batting practice pitch being thrown. One umpire whisked off the plate, while the other straightened out third base. Our manager was holding the scorecard, surveying the players and the field as he wrote down the batting order.

I jumped out of the car, fully dressed except for my spiked shoes. I ran to my position at first base in my white socks, picking up grass stains along the way. As the umpire threw the new ball out to the pitcher, I genuflected to tie my shoes.

The game was tied at 2 by the end of the fifth inning. In the top of the sixth, we went ahead by one. In the bottom of the inning, they tied us and went ahead by two. In our half of the seventh, the last official inning of the game, our first hitter singled and our second hitter homered to tie the game once again. The team was ecstatic.

Then two quick outs followed.

It was my turn to hit. With two balls and two strikes on me, I swung and hit the ball off the end of the bat. It went up in the air into very short right field, eluding the extended reaches of the first and second basemen, bouncing weirdly in front of the right fielder like a squirrel running for cover, which allowed me to reach second base safely.

Our whole team was standing now. The pressure was on the batter and the pitcher and the fielders. The right hit, everyone knew, could send me home with the winning run. The game would end. We would live to play the next round.

Now everything begins to happen in slow motion. There are open mouths and shouting faces, but there are no sounds. Arms are waving. The ball has been hit into the outfield. I'm running in slow motion. I'm racing towards third base in slow motion. I'm looking at my coach. It's Dan. He's raising his arms, but he's not saying anything. There are no sounds anyway. His hands go up. He's going to bless me. No, he's going to give me communion. No, he's waving me home.

The entire team is screaming soundlessly and waving their arms as I pass the third base dugout. The ball is flying towards the catcher, like a white host outlined against the blue sky. The ball and I and the sudden sound of everything happening all arrive together at the exact, precise moment. I slide into the plate, raising an immense dust cloud.

When it settles, I see the umpire with outstretched arms, giving the safe sign.

O Death, where is thy sting!

Heartland

I finally have an office in the house – a small room on the top floor where I am surrounded by books and papers in friendly disarray. I can come up here after dinner with the family, at the end of a long day of negotiating with clients and employees in my business office which is a little more than a mile from my home.

Now that I have a place to put things, I've been gathering them from different storage places in the house.

On top of the bookshelf, I have set out the Hartland figures. When I bought them I believe they cost $1.98 each. I remember saving my money to make a weekly purchase. Now they're considered collectibles.

Each plastic figure stands eight inches tall. They are accurate in likeness and attitude.

Ernie Banks patiently awaits the next pitch.
Stan Musial assumes his distinctive corkscrew stance.
Willie Mays is making a basket catch.
Warren Spahn is mid-windup, hands together above his head.
Mickey Mantle and Roger Maris* swing powerfully from opposite sides of the plate.

Henry Aaron is missing his bat and the brim off his hat was broken through some forgotten act of carelessness.

*Ruth's Homerun Record stood for 34 years before Maris broke it in 1961, but the Maris record lasted for 37 years. This is the real asterisk.

Tickets

I finally found the tickets.

They were two pink stubs in a plastic holder, each marked three dollars. They were dated August 28, 1957. Across the top, in even script, read *Ebbets Field.*

I have two theories about lost things.

The first is that they hide from you. They only let themselves be found when you completely give up looking.

The second theory is that they are jealous creatures. As soon as you begin looking for something else, they suddenly appear.

These hidden things are cunning. Don't think you can trick them by *pretending* to give up the search, or *pretending* to look for something else.

For years I looked for this pair of tickets to the first baseball game I ever attended. I went with my father and an Englishman visiting his company.

I have two visual memories of that evening. There were cameramen with flashbulbs kneeling on one knee in foul territory behind the first baseman; as the runner crossed the base the bulbs would flash.

The second memory is of catcher Roy Campanella leaving his position behind the plate to race towards a runner between first and second base. In my limited experience of the game, I never imagined a catcher could get so involved in the play on the infield.

I also remember that throughout the game, my father tried to explain to the Englishman what was happening on the field.

I remember the Englishman asking, "If they miss it why is it called a strike?"

And I remember my father's answer: "Because they strike at it."

Aside from the fact that the opposing team was the Cubs, I can't say I remember anything else about the game, but an internet site with every modern box score has done a tremendous job of telling me all I that I do not remember.

The Dodgers won the game 4-3, in 14 innings. Sandy Koufax started. He was lifted after the fifth inning. Reliever Ed Roebuck, who won the game, pitched nine innings in relief, certainly something you would not expect to see today. Dale Long of the Cubs hit an inside-the-park home run, that rarest and most exciting of hits, in the fourth inning, scoring the first run of the game. In the bottom of the 14th, Campanella singled to left; Roseboro ran for Campanella and got picked off first base, which must have been a great disappointment; Reese struck out; Jackson, pinch-hitting for Roebuck walked; Gilliam singled, sending Jackson to third; Elmer Valo, pinch-hitting for Gino Cimoli, singled in the game-winning run.

18,019 people were in the stands. And this was the most remarkable thing of all: None of them knew that their beloved Dodgers would only play ten more games in Brooklyn.

Bat and Ball

I don't know how the bat or the ball came into my possession.

All of the autographs on the ball are from members of the 1957 Brooklyn Dodgers. It took some time to decipher them all, but going to the Baseball Almanac online for the 1957 roster and comparing names made the task manageable. Whenever there was any doubt, I shot back to the almanac which almost always showed a baseball card with the player's signature scrawled across it.

Horizontally, across one of the surfaces of the ball where the two seams are closest together, reads: *Walt Alston.*

Here's how the rest of the names are grouped in the longer, oblong panels:

Sandy Amoros
Duke Snider
Pee Wee Reese
Carl Furillo
Rube Walker
Gino Cimoli
Don Bessent

Ed Roebuck
Gil Hodges
Jim Gilliam
Roger Craig
Sandy Koufax
Charley Neal
Don Drysdale

Randy Jackson
Elmer Valo
Don Newcombe
Clem Labine
Danny McDevitt
Don Zimmer

Roy Campanella
Carl Erskine
Johnny Podres

The bat is a solid, thick-handled club, a 35-ounce Louisville slugger, stamped "JR5" on the handle, Jackie Robinson model, *flame-tempered.*

I like to think Mr. Robinson flame-tempered this mysterious bat himself on the field of play.

Swing Music

In 1950,
five hundred ninety-seven at-bats
12 strikeouts.

Alexander the Great

Alexander is a big name for a small boy, only eight years old. Put on your helmet, Alexander, and pick up that club with both hands. It's time to conquer the world.

First and always, never be afraid of the ball.

Look right at the pitcher.

Put on a mean face. This is the one time when a mean face will get you more than a smile, because it lets the pitcher know you mean business.

Your back foot never moves.

As the ball approaches, always step with your front foot towards the pitcher, keeping your hands back as long as possible. Then swing level right through the ball.

If you don't get it this time, you'll get it next time.

This is the greatest game and this is its greatest secret: to be great is to be greater than you were last time. And there will always be a next time.

Winter Ball

It began with a phone call. At the very end of another long business day, my cell phone rang. "Rang" is not the right word. My daughter had recently upgraded my ring tone to the Mission Impossible theme. Finding the phone before it stopped "ringing" became a mission impossible in itself. The sound seemed to be coming from my laptop bag on a chair in the corner of the room. I rifled through too many zippered compartments while the music mockingly continued, but I came up with nothing. Then I turned to the pockets of my jacket. With no time left, I found it and popped it open to hear a voice announcing my mission should I choose to accept it.

There was a baseball game starting in about two hours and a player was needed. Was I interested?

It was the voice of someone in town, someone who had once had an office on the same floor as ours, someone with whom I had played arc softball in the summer. But it was no longer summer; it was the dead of winter, admittedly a mild winter, but the World Series was already a memory. And he was asking about baseball, fast-pitch 90-foot bases baseball, not arc softball, the game of middle-aged men. I hadn't played a real baseball game in more than 20 years.

I had two questions: what was the temperature and how fast should we expect the pitching to be.

"50-60," he said, and "70-80."

He picked me up an hour later. I carried my glove and an old pair of metal spikes. I had on two layers of clothing and a Yankee hat.

"Where is the game?" I asked, as we pulled away.

"New York State," he answered, "just over the border, about half an hour from here."

We talked about the war in Iraq, the price of oil, local goings-on in town as we drove up the parkway into the night. At one extended quiet moment, I looked across at his profile, baseball hat in place, and I had the odd sensation that none of this was what it seemed to be. I felt like a character in a Stephen King story. There was in fact no baseball game in the middle of the winter for players past their prime. I was being brought to a place for people who could not give up certain unconscious desires. My neighbor was one of the delivery men. That's why, over the years, whatever casual conversations we had he would always steer towards baseball; it had all been a test. When we arrived the experiments would begin.

But there was a baseball field. It was well lit. Most of the players were in full uniform. Pitchers were throwing on the sidelines. A catcher was putting on his equipment. An umpire was straightening out third base. Numerous players were stretching and bending and swinging weighted bats. It all felt completely familiar, yet it all felt totally brand new.

I would play first base. The game began instantly. I threw warm-up tosses to the infielders. The ball seemed so small and hard. The first two innings passed without a play for me – all pop-ups to other parts of the field and two strikeouts. I batted for the first time in the bottom of the third inning. My timing was all off. I looked foolish. I was way behind on a fastball and went down on the next two curve balls. I had never seen curve balls like the ones thrown to me.

My second time up I tapped to the mound. The base was far away. I had a few putouts at first and I took a few pick-off throws. First base was the easiest position on the field.

My third time at bat I singled to right over the second baseman's head. It brought in the tying run. The next batter forced me at second. When I came to the bench, people began to talk to me. No one had said a word up until then. They congratulated me and asked my name.

My fourth time up I singled more solidly to right field. We were winning the game now. The bench was jovial. People were slapping me on the back and asking what team I played on and whether I would be there in the spring. I got up once more and hit the ball better than any of the other times, but the left fielder ran it down for an out. This was one of the things about baseball that kept you humble, reminding you that there were other forces at work than yourself, that in the same game you might hit the ball weakly and get on base and hit it extremely well and come up with nothing.

While I was tossing warm-up throws before the top of the ninth, the lights suddenly went out and the game was over.

My neighbor explained to me back in the car that we played nine innings or until 11PM, when the township turned off the lights. Sometimes the man in charge of the switch flipped it early for who knows what reason. That's what happened tonight at 10:35. This gave the game an existential dimension. You played until the lights went out.

This game would have remained a one-time distant memory, if the phone didn't ring again early one Sunday morning in November. This time the voice was more desperate. They needed a player. The game was at a field in northern New Jersey somewhat difficult to find. Without committing to going, I wrote down hurried directions. Twenty minutes later I was in the car; after two cell phone calls about which turn to take, I was stepping onto the field just in the nick of time. I went right to my position at third base only to be greeted by a screaming line drive off the first pitch of the game, which I caught in self-defense.

Everyone seemed genuinely happy just to be there. We were guys in our forties and fifties, and a few in their sixties, playing baseball in the northeastern United States *in November*. There was a clock on the tower above the parking lot, which could be seen from the certain spots on the field. The hands had stopped moving.

While I crouched in my position, the third base coach talked to me: "I'm 53 years old," he said. "I'm retired. There's nothing I'd rather be doing than this."

He would later come in to pitch. In the dugout, he would tell us how he had been a NYC cop for twenty years, that he'd worked undercover in narcotics.

Our first baseman looked like Willie McCovey, except he batted from the right side. His name was Ulysses. "It was my father's middle name and it's my son's middle name." He had a big swing; his weakness was the curve ball, low and outside. But if you missed and left it in his zone, he could hit it a mile.

Our pitcher was a lefty with good stuff. He wore pinstripe pants and a blue Yankee sweatshirt. So far, he had shut out the opposition; we were in the fourth inning.

The opposing catcher was affable. He never stopped talking. "Tell me what pitch you want," he would say while you tried to concentrate. "You want the knuckle curve. Just let me know what you want." They were words you could trust or not trust. The longer we played into the late morning the more real the game became.

A Vida Blue look-alike in his sixties wearing an Oakland Athletics uniform stood behind the backstop holding an unvarnished bat made of reddish wood.

"Take a look at this," he said to me, "offering me the bat. I manufacture these bats," he said. "They're made from a hard wood only found in Africa. See how many major league bats break and splinter these days? These won't."

The batter stuck out. He took the bat from me and went into the cage. He hit the first pitch to the shortstop and legged out the play, all sixty-five years of him.

There was a man keeping score in the dugout. He discussed different acquaintances he had in common with some of the other players. "I'm 76," I heard him say. "I was 71 when I pitched my last game."

"I want to be you," said the retired cop.

After the game, in the parking lot, I learned that he had been a catcher in the Yankee farm system, rumored to have a tremendous arm. He had come up to the majors the same day as Mickey Mantle, only to go back down four days later. It was a story full of tragic details. You could look it up.

When the game ended the players were asked to gather on the mound. A beautiful, young woman with a camera materialized out of nowhere. It was a day for miracles, so why not one more? Each player had paid $10, and the excess money would be donated to a local food pantry for the homeless. The photo that the woman took would appear on the league's website.

We played every Sunday morning through the winter of 2006, except for Christmas Eve. The uncommonly mild weather was on everyone's mind. Scientists predicted that the next year would be the hottest on record. We hoped it had to do with El Nino and not global warming.

Each Sunday we were astonished to find ourselves back on the field, playing the game. On New Year's Eve we couldn't help but recognize that each game was a celebration. The games together were a string of celebrations in which we each played our role like ancient peoples acting out their history.

In the last inning of the New Year's Eve game, our catcher shed his armor and swung his war club like mighty Ajax sending the sphere to distant parts where the center fielder swift-footed, like Mercury, caught it in the air. Tagging up from third base, Ulysses sailed safely home. It was classic.

Reunion

Every summer since my parents passed away we have organized a family reunion at the farmhouse which they left us. My mother was the seventh of ten children and my father the last of five; my siblings and I were born into a tribe.

The tribe has dwindled and grown. The aunts and uncles, pillars of a magnificent structure, are now fewer, while their children and their children's children are so many I no longer know by looking at them to whom they all belong, let alone their names.

Growing up surrounded by so many aunts and uncles, I formed the childhood impression that they represented all of humanity. They were tall and short, thin and not so thin, loud and quiet, cheerful and solemn; obsessed with cleanliness and couldn't care less; deeply religious and couldn't care less; fleshing out every kind of presence and painful degrees of absence – the uncle who moved to California; we would see him rarely and never get to know his family; the uncle who disappeared into the doomed, protracted struggle that began on Anzio beachhead, from whose death the family has never recovered. They all had in common that they could make things with their hands, and that two global events had shaped their lives – the Great Depression and World War II.

From the subtle differences in the tomato sauce served by a dozen aunts and two grandmothers, I learned variations on a theme. To this day, I can't taste anyone's sauce, home-made or restaurant, without locating it on that spectrum. Christmas trees extended the lesson. From house to house we went with wrapped presents. I can still see each family's tree; the same from year to year; but distinct from all of the others; each year standing in the same spot in the same room. The Douglas fir that always touched the ceiling draped with garland everything reaching upward; the fullest scotch pine, tinsel on every inch of every branch, shining balls of color; the balsam fir with wooden ornaments and paper angels, nativity figures made of papier mache; the white pine, with blue needles, the whitest tree of all, snow on its branches, ghostly and majestic.

Each year we go through the back-breaking task of getting the farm ready for the reunion, swearing that this will be the last time, weeding the gardens, cutting the low-hanging branches, cleaning out the barns, arranging the tables and chairs.

Everyone brings some specialty... pasta, baked ziti, shells, lasagna, sausage and peppers, trays of chicken cutlets, massive salads, cannoli, pignoli, home made cream puffs, fruit, nuts, bottles of red wine.

Two of the cousins get into the perennial argument over who handles the grill better and then end up splitting the job. Another cousin brings out a guitar and there is singing, impromptu dancing and endless conversation.

The highlight of the reunion is the baseball game that takes place away from the house on the green stretch of land out back. I cannot walk anywhere on the land without remembering how many flowers grew here in such brilliant color while my mother was there to tend them, or how many fruit trees and bushes – peaches and plums and berries of all kinds.

The place is still vibrantly green, though. We fashion a field defined by makeshift bases. There is no age or gender restriction; this is a democratic game. The younger boys and the older girls are the most serious players. They hit the ball as hard as they can, run as fast as they can, take the extra base. The boys make heroic, diving catches and keep strict score while no one else is counting.

When I'm up my biggest fear is hitting one of the children with a line drive, so I take it very easy.

Uncle Sam, my mother's youngest brother, now in his seventies, surveys his fielders, then turns back to peer intently at the catcher. Slowly, he brings his hands over his head into a full windup. He pitches. His two grandsons, both left-handers under ten years old, bat against him, one after the other. Each gets a solid hit and races gleefully out of the imaginary box.

"See what Grandpa taught you," he says. "He taught you good."

We are four generations playing a timeless game on a green field. I am one of them.

10 o'clock

A group of families with children of similar ages moved into summer houses on the island at just about the same time. There was a softball field in the town, and the young men met there on Sunday mornings to play double-headers. They favored the ten o'clock pitching motion, so named because it compares the pitcher's arms to the hands on a clock. During his delivery, the pitcher can reach back and raise his arm no higher than ten o'clock. It was also called modified fast pitch softball. The men liked it because it was as close as they could get to actually playing baseball within the confines of the field.

They met summer after summer, and soon their boys wanted to join in the game. When the boys got a little older they also got bolder, and instead of playing alongside their fathers, they wanted to play against them -- sons against fathers.

The fathers were amused by this. They were proud that their sons had challenged them. They felt it was a step in the right direction.

To give the boys a fighting chance, the men batted the opposite way. If a father was right-handed, he batted left-handed; if he was left-handed, he batted right-handed.

Suddenly, when the boys reached a certain age, they all seemed to decide independently that the place where they had spent so many memorable summers, with its balmy air and beautiful beaches, was no longer the place to be.

The boys disappeared from the island.

The men returned to their usual Sunday games against each other. They had become a little slower in the field. They joked about aches and pains, but none of them had lost the love of playing.

One by one, as they reached a certain age, the boys began to return to the island. They were handsome young men now, tall and strong.

When they had enough players to field a team, the sons challenged their fathers just as they had when they were young boys.

To give the old men a fighting chance, the sons batted the opposite way.

Mr. November

Where were the ticket scalpers? They were everywhere before every game. At playoff and World Series time, they would be unusually hopped up, waving their wares, conspiratorial and out in the open at once, an odd mixture. But now, on our walk from the parking lot to the stadium they were nowhere to be seen.

And there was this odd absence of sound. Even before the least important game, a river of chatter flowed from the fans as they moved towards the ticket gates. The more exuberant shouted and banged against the plastic walls of the caterpillar walkway.

But not tonight.

Tonight we filed into the stadium in utter silence. I could only compare it to how we sometimes left the place after a terrible loss, each absorbed in thought, thinking the same thoughts.

We were here tonight because to be here was part of our normal lives, and to try to forget for a few hours what had happened, but the silence kept reminding us that we were not doing a very good job of forgetting.

It didn't help that our team was behind, 2 games to 1.

When you enter the stadium, the green of the field greets you in an overwhelming rush. The greenness is in such remarkable contrast to the concrete world from which you have just stepped that it commands all of your attention. Then history surrounds you; it descends from the rows upon rows of blue seats to embrace you.

This happens every time; you may think that you notice it less the more often you go, but it's always there. To be reminded, you just have to bring someone who has never been to the stadium before. It doesn't even have to be a baseball fan.

But this time was different. This time there were armed men in the stands. They wore army fatigues and carried machine guns. We knew why they were here; we hoped that their presence did not mean that our world had changed forever.

My son stood at my side. He was thirteen years old. He had been coming with me to games since the age of six. We had seen some great ones together. We sat through a rain-soaked fifteen-inning marathon against Seattle in 1995, when he was only seven years old, which ended with a game-winning home-run. Through that night, I kept asking him if he'd had enough, did he want to go home, but he steadfastly answered no until the famous hit ended the game.

We saw exciting playoff and World Series games through the years, and what seemed like hundreds of regular season games, but none could compare with what would take place tonight.

I remembered going to a handful of games with my father. Each one was an event. From where we parked, we would walk through three or four baseball fields in the shadow of the stadium where young men in uniforms were playing serious baseball. For years as a child I thought that these fields so close to the stadium were the minor leagues. If you played well enough you were promoted to the majors – every player's dream – and you walked through the gates onto the stadium field.

Just last week, six years from that memorable game, I am speeding through the television channels to find a Yankee game, but I don't realize it's an off-day. Instead, I find myself watching a classic replay of that night. It's the eighth inning; the score is 3-1 in favor of the Diamondbacks. Byung-Hyun Kim, the Arizona closer has just taken the mound.

He proceeds to strike out Spencer, Brosius, and Soriano. Things are not looking good. As the drama unfolds on the television screen, I project myself back into the crowd. If weariness can be new, we were living on that day with a new feeling of weariness. Not quite shock anymore, as it had been in the first few hours, through the first day or even the first week, but a new awareness of the world and ourselves, previously inconceivable, twisted around the undeniable fact that we were still standing here to feel it, and others were not.

At this point in every game, my son and I would move from our seats between third base and home plate to the right side of the stadium which is closer to the lot where we park the car. It doesn't mean we leave before the last pitch, only that we can exit quickly once it is thrown. We crossed to the other side of the stadium.

Now, I'm looking back at the television, which has skipped past the uneventful top of the Arizona inning to the bottom of the ninth. I remember we are standing in the aisle even with first base. There are no empty seats.

Jeter leads off the inning with a bunt down the third base line; he is thrown out. Two outs left. Paul O'Neill steps into the box. He delivers a single to left; as he rounds the base our hopes are raised. Bernie can do it. He's done it so many times before. But not this time; Bernie goes down on strikes.

We are all fighting the same feeling that something has changed, irrevocably. That things are being taken away from us, one by one. That New York is a different city. We don't want to believe it. We look past the policemen to the soldiers, strategically placed in the stands. Somehow we are down to our last out.

Tino steps up.

I know what happens next, but I watch it happen again on the screen. The ball leaves his bat in unbelievable flight. It takes a micro-second before the crowd understands. The game is tied. Everyone's screaming. I'm screaming. I see my son high five-ing a soldier with a machine gun.

Two more runners reach base that inning, but the Yankees fail to score. We go into the tenth inning.   It is Halloween night.

Jeter steps in.   The clock strikes midnight, moving the game into November for the first time in major league history.

I am glued to the screen as if to the climactic scene in a movie no less compelling however many times I see it.

It's different than a movie, though, because the images on the screen awaken the sensations of actually having been there when the real thing took place – the night air, the sounds, the feelings.

Kim gets two quick strikes on Jeter; then throws a ball. He fouls off the next two pitches. Then he takes two more balls for a full count. He sends the next ball down the right field line solidly, but clearly foul; every eye in the stadium follows the ball.

Then it happens.

The pitch comes in; the ball goes out into the night, up, up, over the wall.

It is as if 50,000 strangers jumped together, on an infinite, invisible box spring, up and down, deliriously shouting and leaning on each other for minutes that lasted hours.   One of them waved a sign that said, "Mr. November."

The shouting did not stop. And no one left. They stood, noisy and stunned, unwilling to move, wrenching as much joy as they could from the moment, released from their grim reflections as long as they could make it last.

The manager beckoned the mayor onto the field of celebration. It was fitting.

∞

9 innings
4 bases
3 outs
1 game